WHERE'S THE POO?

ORCHARD

ORCHARD BOOKS

First published in Great Britain in 2019

by The Watts Publishing Group

9 10

© 2019 The Watts Publishing Group Limited

Illustrations by Dynamo Limited

Additional images © Shutterstock

A CIP catalogue record for this book is available from the British Library

ISBN 978 1 40835 964 8

Printed and bound in China

MIX
Paper from
responsible sources
FSC
www.fsc.org   FSC® C104740

Orchard Books
An imprint of Hachette Children's Group
Part of The Watts Publishing Group Limited
Carmelite House
50 Victoria Embankment
London EC4Y 0DZ

An Hachette UK Company
www.hachette.co.uk

WHERE'S THE POO?

FLUSHED AWAY!

Have you ever wondered what happens to the poos that you do? Well now you can see exactly what they get up to once they've gone down the pan!

These number twos won't pass up the chance for some fun. They are ready to go with the flow and see where the next flush takes them!

Can you spot them all on their adventure? The answers are at the back of the book, along with some extra things to look out for!

RAINBOW ROY
Brightly coloured, this poo stands out among his natural friends!

QUEENIE
Queenie is the poo in charge. You can find her on her porcelain throne!

BOBBI
A cosy hat keeps Bobbi warm on journeys down the drain.

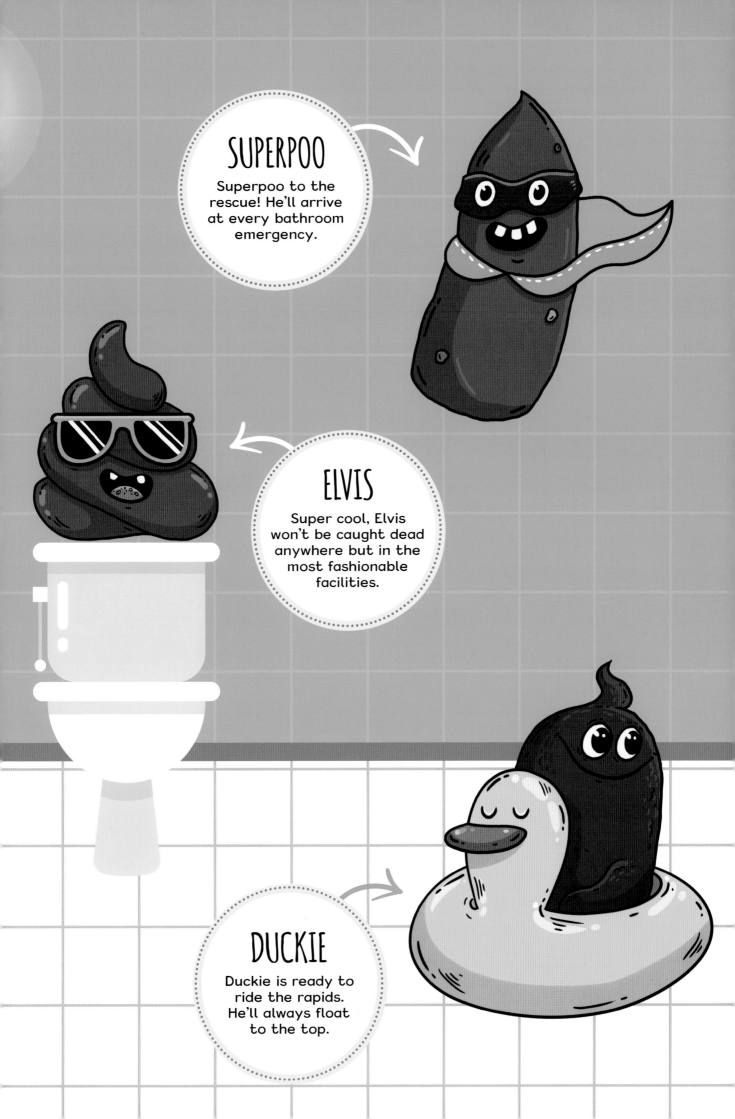

AQUARIUM

The poos see a lot on their underground travels but they've never seen so many amazing sea creatures!

SAFARI

Amongst all these animals, the poos aren't worried about being spotted!

TOWN CENTRE

The poos love hanging out in cafes and taking in the sights of the town.

DISCO

Under the bright lights the poos love to strut their stuff and show off their moves.

SEASIDE

The next stop for the gang is a beautiful beach. Time to top up their tan!

AIRPORT

Normally travelling underground, the poos can't wait to be high fliers!

RAINFOREST

In the rainforest, the poos fit right in. Maybe they'll make some new friends!

WATER PARK

The poos can't wait to try out all the slides. Last one down is the loser!

ROLLER DISCO

Let's roll! The poos are ready for a spin around the dance floor.

GALLERY

The poos are excited to see the fossils. Maybe they'll see some of their ancestors!

CLASSROOM

Time to learn!
The poos are ready
to soak up as much
knowledge as they can.

RIVER RAPIDS

After being flushed away, the poos got caught in the rapids. Ready for a wild ride?

DINER

The poos have popped into the diner for a bite to eat. Everyone loves a fast food joint!

THEME PARK

The poos are looking for a thrill at the theme park. Hold tight, everyone!

ANSWERS

Now try and find these extra items in every scene!

AQUARIUM

A red crab	☐
A slippery eel	☐
A man with an ice cream	☐
A woman with sunglasses on her head	☐
A boy touching a starfish	☐
A purple octopus	☐
A man wearing dungarees	☐
A toothy shark	☐
A fish with a light on its head	☐
A boy with a fish on his T-shirt	☐

SAFARI

Two men taking a picture	☐
A leaping frog	☐
A monkey having a bath	☐
A yawning hippo	☐
Three baby elephants	☐
A bird standing on a rhino	☐
A monkey climbing a tree	☐
A man using binoculars	☐
A monkey hitching a ride	☐
A red flag	☐

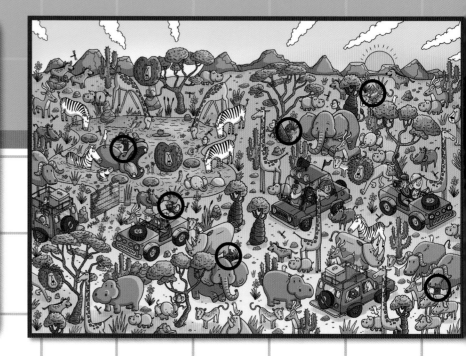

TOWN CENTRE

A big slice of pizza ☐

A woman putting on lipstick ☐

A boy with a teddy bear ☐

A football ☐

A man reading a newspaper ☐

A dog sitting down ☐

A boy on a scooter ☐

A cat on a ledge ☐

A woman with a walking frame ☐

A man walking a dog ☐

DISCO

A pregnant woman ☐

A man in a suit and green shirt ☐

A DJ ☐

A woman in a lime green dress ☐

Six red balloons ☐

A man wearing a red baseball cap ☐

A boy with a dinosaur on his T-shirt ☐

Musical notes ☐

A boy wearing a bow tie ☐

Two purple drinks ☐

SEASIDE

- A man playing the guitar ☐
- A starfish balloon ☐
- A crab ☐
- A man surfing ☐
- A woman knitting ☐
- A boy buried in sand ☐
- A girl building a sandcastle ☐
- A man with a green mohawk ☐
- A girl jumping in to the sea ☐
- A girl throwing a bucket of water ☐

AIRPORT

- A man with an anchor tattoo ☐
- Two men reading a newspaper ☐
- A woman with sunglasses on her head ☐
- A cup of coffee ☐
- A man wearing a straw hat ☐
- A woman holding a passport ☐
- A boy crying ☐
- A picture of a palm tree ☐
- A man wearing purple headphones ☐
- A girl sitting on a pink suitcase ☐

RAINFOREST

A man in a spotty hat ☐

A sloth holding a tree trunk ☐

A lemur having a bath ☐

Two coconuts in a tree ☐

A man standing on a rock ☐

Four pink flamingoes ☐

A monkey hanging from a tree ☐

A woman wearing a red hat ☐

Three sleeping tigers ☐

A man with purple shorts ☐

WATER PARK

A lifeguard ☐

A slice of watermelon ☐

A donut inflatable ☐

A man having a shower ☐

Three birds sitting in a row ☐

A sign for ice cream ☐

A flask ☐

Two pizza inflatables ☐

Two rackets ☐

A red football ☐

CLASSROOM

- A boy playing hopscotch ☐
- A painting of a dinosaur ☐
- A girl lying on a beanbag ☐
- A girl carrying red paint ☐
- A girl with a sun on her T-shirt ☐
- A girl with her feet on the table ☐
- Spilt blue paint ☐
- A clock ☐
- A boy with his hand up ☐
- A boy kneeling on a chair ☐

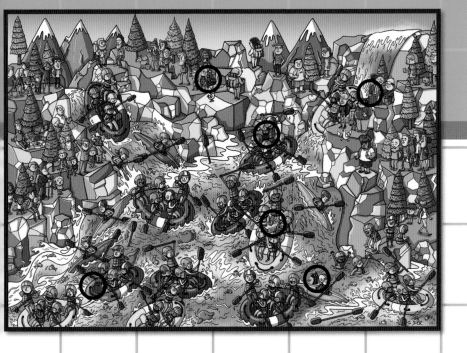

RIVER RAPIDS

- A man having a picnic ☐
- A cat ☐
- A white football ☐
- A man looking through binoculars ☐
- A boy wearing a blue cap ☐
- Three dogs ☐
- A woman holding a cup ☐
- A man with a long white beard ☐
- Two seagulls ☐
- A woman holding a baby ☐

DINER

An ice cream sundae ☐

A jukebox ☐

Six waiters on rollerskates ☐

A gold disc ☐

A woman eating a hamburger ☐

A napkin dispenser ☐

Five plates of salad ☐

A woman putting ketchup on a hot dog ☐

A man drinking through a straw ☐

A man holding a knife and fork ☐

THEME PARK

A green-faced witch ☐

A man eating a hot dog ☐

A clown ☐

A seagull ☐

A unicorn balloon ☐

A man with a skull on his T-shirt ☐

A boy eating candyfloss ☐

A girl dressed as a superhero ☐

A werewolf ☐

A woman reading a map ☐